CREATING AN A+ CLASSROOM

by BILL BAILEY

A HANDS-ON, NO NONSENSE, PRACTICAL GUIDE
FOR TEACHERS WHO WANT TO CREATE
AND MAINTAIN AN EFFECTIVE A+ CLASSROOM

Plus
UNIQUE TIPS, TECHNIQUES, HINTS AND MORE

CHARACTER PRESS
MASON, OHIO

For information about booking Bill Bailey, contact:

Bill Bailey Productions, Inc.
310-316-8655
www.billbaileyproductions.com

email: billbaileyspeaks@aol.com

This book may be purchased in bulk at discount for educational uses. Contact Character Press. Inquiries should be addressed to:

Character Press c/o The Character Institute
7577 Central Parke Blvd. Suite 217
Mason, OH 45040
513-229-3626

**the
character institute**

Published by
The Character Institute

Edited by
Bill Bailey Productions, Inc.

Cover and Inside Design
Aimee Sposito Martini

Printed in the United States of America

1st edition

ISBN 0-9772017-0-8

To Betsy. . .

my best friend, my soul mate, my love, my wife.
Because of your support, love, and encouragement,
I found the strength to follow my dreams. You're
the source of all my happiness. Thank you for
giving us Bridgie, and for saying, "I do."

CREATING AN A+ CLASSROOM

Contents

Acknowledgments

SPECIAL THANKS to Curtis Zimmerman . . . my other best friend. Thank you for pointing me in the right direction and encouraging me to reach a little further. We've come a long way since 1977, and the journey just keeps getting better. We're definitely living the dream. I love you, brother!

The following people have made a significant difference in my life. THANK YOU!

Helen Bailey
Vic Bailey
Jay Bailey
Bella Allan
William Allan
Jim Bailey
Vicky Newcomb
Dee Reitzall
Dick Honrath
Father Glenn
Steve Schafer
Sister St. Michael
Father Pascual
Lynn Irvin
Helen Patterson
Dave Brulette
Bill Bailey, Jr.
Dr. Tom Gibbs
Georgianne Green
Gerald Locklin
John McFall
Georgia Marshall
George Becker

Al Goodman
Moira Leigh
Dave O'Brien
Heather Newcomb
Holly Turek
Heidi Newcomb
Martha Shaw
Betsy Bailey
Betty Herring
Jack Herring
Lynn Zebley
Brent Foster
Dave Katz
Bridgie Bailey
Don Todd
Louie Pastor
Jennifer Bailey
Karen Mohr
James Briscoe
Kennedy Bailey
Griffin Bailey
John Silk

Introduction

Congratulations! You have made a conscious choice to enter a world where you will have a profound impact on the lives of many students. And for that, I applaud you.

For over thirty years I made my living as a middle-school teacher and as an activities director. I prided myself on being the best, most effective teacher I could be. It was by far much more than just a job . . . it was an adventure. An adventure that gave me a great deal of satisfaction and challenge every day of my life. But an adventure that I was clearly committed to, and one that most assuredly required my dedication, my compassion, and my desire to be a positive role model for the children I was hired to teach.

Now it's your turn.

Teaching, like any respected profession, isn't mastered overnight. It takes planning and preparation, a constant desire to be good at what you do, a willingness to learn from your mistakes and make adjustments, a love to work and share with other people, and an incredible sense of intention and focus. The career you've chosen requires intelligence, diligence, integrity, tons of patience, discipline, an open mind, a sense of humor, leadership, and most importantly, understanding. This book was designed for you, the soon-to-be or new teacher. Spread out through these pages is my "bag of tricks" that I picked up over the last 30 years. It's the same bag I've shared with hundreds of teachers in workshops across the country. I'm sure you master teachers out there will find some value also.

I know this information will help you become the best teacher you can be. But ultimately the choice is yours. Just remember . . . if you're happy and enjoy what you do each day, then your students will be happy learning as well.

Keep your eyes and mind open, laugh as often as you can (*maybe not the first week*), and never, ever forget that what you do each day changes lives. Enjoy teaching.

1988

There's only one marshal in this town.

① Set the Tone

Set the tone you want for the entire year on Day 1.
The minute the students first set foot in your room
they should get a sense for how things will go in
the months ahead. Keep in mind that they are
children who are both nervous and excited about
their new schedules. Therefore, what you say and
what you do that first day can have a lasting
impression. So, set a positive tone early.

1. Greet the students at the door.
(How you doin? No, how YOU doin?)

Whether you have the students line up, or you
allow the students to come right in, make an effort
to greet them as they enter your room.

This is an important component of an
effective classroom for the following reasons:

- You set the tone you want immediately.

- You can eliminate unacceptable behavior at
the door.

- You have an opportunity early on to positively
reinforce a student who otherwise might be a
behavior problem.

- You can direct their attention to a warm-up
assignment or notes you have on the board.

- You can reinforce classroom rules, such as,
"All students should have necessary materials
(*i.e. paper, pen or pencil, book, and homework*)
on their desks before the final bell".

- You can put a smile on a student's face who
may be otherwise having a bad day.

2. Assign seats the first day.
(Table for one? Right this way.)

When students arrive at school the first day, they
are excited, nervous, and eager to learn. What they
don't need or appreciate the first day is having to
make a lot of choices. So, have your seating chart

or seating activity ready to go and in place. This accomplishes three things:

1. You immediately send the message that you are in control and have a plan.

2. It allows you more time to discuss what's really important.

3. You have a seating chart in which you can take roll and begin memorizing names.

I have used and observed many different ways to seat students the first day. They range from seating students alphabetically to alternating boy-girl-boy-girl to having the students choose a card or number that corresponds to a seat with that card or number in the classroom. Regardless of what technique you use, my advice to you is to definitely have a seating plan.

Card Trick

You'll need two decks of cards. Based on the number of seats you have in your classroom, peel off that number of cards from the first deck. That's right, all the cards won't be used. Discard all the cards you don't need. Do the same with the second deck – keep the cards that match with the first deck and discard the rest.

Shuffle both decks several times. Using only the first deck, tape one card to the corner of each desk.

Now you're set. As you greet the students at the door, give each of them a card from the second deck. They are to find the seat that corresponds with the card they're holding. It's easy, it's fun, and it's effective. If you teach more than one class in that room, don't forget to collect the cards from the students so you can use them with the next class or period.

Make a seating chart based on the results and you're done.

VARIATIONS ON A THEME:
1. 3x5 cards work great if you don't want to use playing cards.

2. Using two sets of 3x5 cards, you can use:
    ▭ A. numbers
    ▭ B. letters (*you might have to also use double letters*)
    ▭ C. colors
    ▭ D. body parts
    ▭ E. character traits

LET'S GET REALLY CRAZY:
Place a 3x5 card on every desk before the students come in. As they enter, let them sit anywhere. Have them put their name and month they were born on the cards and pass them forward to you. Then have all the students stand and move to the back. Starting with January, or backwards with December, seat the students according to the months they were born.

It doesn't matter which technique you use to seat your students, but make sure you have one for the first day.

3. Learn your students' names
(You can call me Ray, or you can call me Ray Ray).

I don't think it helps your program any if by the third week you're still pointing to students because you don't know their names. It's uncomfortable and impersonal, and it can also be embarrassing.

You can eliminate this scenario by learning their names. The quicker you memorize their names *(at least their first name)*, the sooner they'll feel comfortable in your class and the faster they'll buy into your program and begin learning.

Quicker   Sooner   Faster

TRY THIS!

I used to make a contest out of memorizing their names. I'd tell them, "If I don't have your first names memorized by such and such a day (*you decide*), then everyone gets a treat." If you want to save money on candy, then memorize their names. Plus, it reinforces the importance of memorization.

Q "Nothing great was ever achieved without enthusiasm."
                                                    -Ralph Waldo Emerson

NOTES

WILLIAM ANDERSON
SCHOOL
MR. BAILEY
GRADE 6
1974-75

1974

It seems like it was just yesterday.

② My First Day

As any new employee can tell you, the first day on
the job can be nerve racking. Call it a combination
of excitement and anxiety, there's a good chance no
one gets much sleep the night before.

For me it was no different. I was hired to teach
6th grade three days before the opening of the
1974-75 school year. But that was common practice
then. There was a glut of teachers and very few
openings. I was very lucky, and very, very nervous.
That weekend I worked all day Saturday in my
classroom, and on Sunday I worked all day until
well past midnight planning lessons and what I
would say on Monday. Of course, I had no appetite.
If that wasn't enough to worry about, I had one

other major concern for my first day. . . my son Bill was starting first grade at the same school. As you can imagine, he was also stressed. On the one hand, he was excited because he was going to get to go to the same school as Dad. But, on the other hand, he was very scared because he was not going back to a school he'd been attending for the last 3 years, and he had been their favorite student.

As we pulled into the parking lot, I was thinking I didn't feel that well. I looked over at Bill and he was starting to cry. We walked together that September day holding hands, moments away from entering the unknown. Two men ready to face the next challenge together.

I checked into the office, picked up my paperwork, and then walked him to his new room. His new teacher, Mrs. Kaku, met us at the door and immediately sized up the situation. She said, "OK Billy, say goodbye to Dad – he has a class waiting for him." It took everything I had not to cry as I watched my little big man being escorted into his classroom. He was looking back over his shoulder and the look on his face said, "Dad, please don't leave me."

Suddenly, a bell rang and I realized I had a class waiting for me. I took a deep breath and raced to the auditorium. An aide at the door stopped me and said, "Mr. Bailey, your little angels are waiting for you at the front right table. You may take them to class now."

When I got to the table I took a moment to look at the 28 faces that were to become my first and most memorable class. Then I smiled and said, "Good morning. My name is Mr. Bailey and I'll be your teacher this year for 6th grade. I don't know if you know this or not, but you've been hand picked to be in the best class at Anderson Elementary. Now, everyone stand, form two lines, and let's walk quietly to Room 15."

I had 29 other "first days" during my career as a teacher . . . some I remember, most I've forgotten. Not that I didn't enjoy them, I did. It's just that they've become a bit fuzzy. Yet, my first day in 1974 is as clear as if it happened yesterday. It's funny about "firsts". . . they're exciting and scary and memorable. For me, my first day set the tone for the caliber of passion and commitment I would exude for the next 30 years.

NOTES

③ Be Consistent

Being consistent is probably one of the most important characteristics of effective teaching and good parenting. Children (*students*) need to know that what you say, you mean. If you state there'll be a big test every Friday, then you need to make sure you give that test every Friday. If not turning in homework means getting detention, then you need to make sure that every student who didn't have his/her homework gets detention. Consistency and follow-through help students organize, plan, and focus.

1. Put the agenda for the day on the board.
(Today's Specials)

We have all been to many conferences and workshops. The best always list the agenda for the morning or for that session. That puts everyone on the same page as to what's going to be covered that day. It sets the tone and lays out the direction. It also lets everyone know what will be expected of them.

It's the same for your students. They always want to know what they're going to be doing that day. It's a starting point, and it alleviates stress. It also eliminates Jason asking every day, "So, what are we going to be doing today?" Now you can start each class or period with a smile.

(EXAMPLE)

Today's Agenda
- A. Copy notes
- B. Read story, "Thank you, "M'am"
- C. Answer questions on p. 79
- D. Review speech topics

2. Collect homework on the day it's due.

Period. If you don't, you penalize the students who want to do the right thing and who care. Also, you have rewarded those students who don't care. You have suddenly jeopardized the program you have worked hard to build. You're telling your students that deadlines don't matter.

Remember, homework should be assigned for three reasons:

1) additional practice for a lesson you have recently taught
2) information they'll need for a lesson you'll introduce the next day, or
3) reviewing skills they need to revisit so that they'll be prepared for an upcoming test.

Homework should not be assigned as punishment or because you think giving busy work makes you an effective teacher.

EFFECTIVE TEACHERS:
- assign homework

- collect homework on the due date

- reward good homework habits

3. Test students on what you've taught.

Your lesson is well planned. You've introduced your students to the material and important concepts of the lesson, and you've provided adequate time for understanding and questions. You've also built in time for review and some pop quizzes. Now it's time to test them to see if they've grasped those concepts and truly understand the objectives your lesson was designed to achieve.

Of course, that's what a valid test hopes to achieve. The scores should honestly reflect what has been learned based on what has been taught. Don't expect your students to perform well on a test that requires them to answer questions or perform tasks on material you either didn't cover or on material you didn't cover adequately. Would you like that to happen to you? I think not.

An effective teacher designs a test that accurately reflects what's been taught. That way the teacher can assess who's getting it, who's not getting it, which students need additional assistance, and when it's time to move on.

4. Return graded assignments in a reasonable amount of time.

Students need feedback on how they're doing. Returning graded material in a reasonable amount of time rewards students who are working hard, and who are trying to improve. Students thrive, learn, and grow in a consistent, well-organized learning environment.

Q "The only place where success comes before work is in the dictionary." -Vidal Sassoon

④ The Four R's

When I entered the teaching profession, I was reminded of the three R's: reading, writing, and arithmetic. As a new teacher, I immediately saw the importance of teaching and reinforcing these three academic areas each day as part of my primary curriculum.

However, one thing always bothered me: two of the words don't begin with the letter R. Now, aside from the fact I get the sound thing, I felt something more was needed for today's new teacher. So, I created the four R's:

- Readiness
- Rules
- Routine
- Reflection

Today's educators must not only have a precise understanding of their academic specialty and how to teach it, but they must also have a pretty good understanding of their audience (*their students*), how their students learn, how to motivate and inspire their students, and lastly, how to edit or change their program so they can reach the largest number of students

Quicker   Sooner   Faster.

The Four R's

READINESS
- Mental, physical and emotional preparation
- Prepare the necessary materials (*i.e. classroom, first day, beginning a project*)
- Lesson plans
- Room arrangement (*i.e. bulletin boards, seating chart, access to support materials*)

RULES
- Organization
- Communication
- Classroom discipline plan (*i.e. expectations, rules, consequences, rewards*)
- Parents return copy signed

ROUTINE
- Consistency
- Accountability
- Review
- Parent contacts
- Documentation
- Student folders

REFLECTION
- Evaluation (*both teacher and students*)
- Keep a journal
- Looking back (*i.e. what worked and what wasn't effective*)
- Looking forward (*i.e. planning for the next year or next project*)

All you need is a little courage.

⑤ Be Enthusiastic

Enough said. Right? I mean, if you aren't excited about the lesson, activity, or book that you're teaching, then how in the world can you expect your students to be. Granted, everyone has an occasional bad day (*including your students*), but you deal with it or get through it and move on. But a vital characteristic of all effective teachers is that they're fired up about what they're teaching. Effective teachers know that there is a direct correlation between their commitment and enthusiasm, and the number of students who ultimately become actively engaged and make the extra effort to want to learn and be successful. Everyone say, "AMEN."

Learning is fun, and it should be a lifelong pursuit.

I mean, after all, it's next to impossible to learn everything and there's barely enough time to learn about everything you want. So, make learning fun and exciting. It's a win-win proposition.

Every day with every class I opened with an interesting fact or anecdote or quote that I found intriguing or thought-provoking. It was always tied in with the theme or concept I was presenting that day. If nothing else, it gave the students a starting point that captured their attention immediately, and, at the same time, gave me an audience that was focused and ready to transition into the lesson for that day.

Q "The absence of spirit is apathy."
-Bill Bailey

⑥ Sell, Sell, Sell!

Any successful CEO or director or real estate
agent will tell you the same basic principle: if you
don't get excited about what you truly believe is
important and valued, then no one else will either.

It's pretty simple. You possess an item or items
that other people want or need, and you want them
to have said items. Then, SELL IT! You want your
students to understand and utilize synonyms and
antonyms, then sell them. Find stories, poems, and
articles that use them, plaster them all over your
classroom, and require the students to hunt them
down in magazines, books, the internet, and TV.
I'm sure you're familiar with the movie *Field of
Dreams*. If you build it, they will come.

It doesn't matter whether it's teaching them their
times tables or exposing them to the elements of a
short story or requiring them to be proactive in
your class and raise their hands more . . . it's sell,
sell, SELL.

If it's truly important that your students learn
particular concepts, terms, ideologies, etc., then
you must plan, organize, and sell what you believe
is truly important for them to learn. If you're
excited about what you're teaching, then your
students will get excited, too.

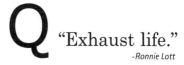

Q "Exhaust life."
-Ronnie Lott

NOTES

1986

"We're on a mission from God!"

⑦ Have a Clear Discipline Plan

A good discipline plan usually includes specific behaviors you expect in your class so that you can teach and your students can learn. It's usually not rocket science, but it does entail sitting down before the school year begins and deciding exactly what the rules should be in your classroom.

I can venture to say most students, and most people for that matter, were raised with some set of rules. Rules help keep people, especially students, focused on making better decisions, and ultimately give themselves a chance to learn and grow.

Like in sports, rules help everyone to enjoy the experience, and at the same time, ensure that everyone has the same chance to grow, be challenged, and succeed.

Remember, students cannot learn, grow, and create in chaos. Students cannot be expected to read and appreciate reading in a noisy environment. A clear discipline plan sets the boundaries for unacceptable behavior and, at the same time, opens the gates for continued learning.

1. Post your classroom rules where all students and guests can see them.

Go over your classroom rules, consequences, and rewards with your class or classes every day the first week. Give examples and take your time, but make sure almost every student understands the rules of the game. I said "almost every student" because on any given day someone is not paying attention or having a bad day or temporarily visiting another reality. So make sure you visit your rules (a.k.a. what you expect from students daily) every day with each class the first week, and at least once a week with each class you teach from then on.

EXAMPLE

Classroom Rules
▢ A. Be on time to class.
▢ B. Don't do anything that prevents another
    student from learning.
▢ C. Have your materials and homework on
    the desk when the bell rings.
▢ D. Begin daily activity as outlined in the
    agenda on the board.

TIP

You'll receive new students throughout the year. Make sure
either you or a student T.A. reviews the rules of your class
with them. See that they get all the necessary papers and
make sure the important ones are signed and returned by a
due date. Make an appointment with each new student ASAP
for a quick conference after school or before lunch. This way
you'll make sure they are welcomed to the class, and have an
opportunity to have any questions answered or their concerns
addressed. It also reinforces the direction of the class.

I was continually talking up the importance of doing our best,
team spirit, and setting and reaching our goals. All new
students who entered my class were immediately welcomed,
and informed that they had been scheduled into the best class
in the school. At the beginning of the year the other students
would chuckle and be amused. By the end of the trimester,
they were nodding and reaching out to those new students.

IF YOUR SON OR DAUGHTER WERE TO SUDDENLY BE
PLACED IN YOUR CLASS, WHAT KIND OF CLASSROOM
WOULD THEY EXPERIENCE?

2. Discuss your discipline plan with all your students.

Most people want to know what's expected of them, whether it be in the workplace or in a relationship. It eliminates the unnecessary stress of guessing, and it also gives everyone involved some indicator as to how they are doing.

Most discipline plans consist of Rules, Expectations, Consequences, and Rewards (*see below*). Give each student a copy of your plan and go over it with them every day the first week. Make sure they take it home, review it with their parents, and return it by a specific date with the parents' signature. Insist that they keep your discipline plan in their folder all year.

CLASSROOM MANAGEMENT

"Rules and consequences and rewards . . . oh my!"

Rules usually reflect a combination of what you want, what the school wants, and what students need. Regardless of the origin, have them . . . and follow through with consequences when they're broken.

Post the rules where all students can see them and review them regularly.

Children need boundaries, and a real clear understanding of what's acceptable and what's not acceptable. When they step across these boundaries or intentionally break a classroom rule, they need to know there are consequences for their actions.

IT'S CALLED DISCIPLINE

LEARN IT, LIVE IT, LOVE IT!

(EXAMPLE)

Classroom Discipline Plan

RULES:
- ▢ A. Be on time to class.
- ▢ B. Don't do anything that prevents another student from learning.
- ▢ C. Have your materials and homework on the desk when the bell rings.
- ▢ D. Begin daily activity as outlined in the agenda on the board.

CONSEQUENCES:
- ▢ A. a warning
- ▢ B. after-school detention and call parent
- ▢ C. after-school detention and an office referral
- ▢ D. parent conference

REWARDS:
- ⬭ Attain skills necessary to be successful in the job world.
- ⬭ Congratulations! By following the rules, you have not only increased your chances of being successful, you've increased your classmates' chances of being successful as well.
- ⬭ All classes that complete all assignments by Friday, and who consistently show support and kindness for all students throughout the week will get special games and surprises for the last half of the period/class on Friday.

ALWAYS
- Be fair
- Be consistent
- Be forgiving

Q "It's a great life if you don't weaken."
-John Buchan

(*Growing up I heard my mother say this quote almost every week.*)

NOTES

1982

Teaching's not a job ... it's an adventure.

⑧ Maintain a Safe Environment

From the moment the first student enters your classroom to the last student who leaves at the end of the day, you are legally responsible for all your students' safety and well-being. That may seem like a great deal of responsibility, and you're right, it is.

You cannot ever lose sight of what's going on in your classroom. Even after you've trained your students on the do's and don'ts of proper classroom behavior, you're still responsible and must always use those "eyes in the back of your head."

I found the following procedures to be very effective:

1) Teach your students the acceptable way to enter and leave your classroom.

2) Position yourself at the door or near the door when the students enter and exit your classroom.

3) Teach your students the acceptable way to use materials (*i.e. scissors, glue, etc.*).

4) Never step out of the classroom for any reason, especially if your students are engaged in a "get out of your seat" type project or activity.

5) Reinforce and reward students who display good safe behavior.

6) Constantly reinforce the importance of working together and looking out for one another.

Familiarize yourself with the school's EMERGENCY PLAN before there's an emergency.

GREAT IDEA!

1983

"What do you mean it's not dress-up day?"

⑨ Be Firm Yet Fair

If your classroom were a business, then you'd be
the CEO. If it were a ship, then you'd be the
captain. The responsibility of getting the job
done or reaching a set goal lies squarely on your
shoulders. You set the tone, the direction, and
the bar.

Being firm means being definite and clear . . . a
person the students can count on that when you
say something, you mean it. Let's say, for example,
you state to your class, "All students who return
their final exam tomorrow signed by their parent
will receive a free homework pass." Being firm and
fair means you follow through with no exceptions.

An effective teacher is an effective leader, and an effective leader is always firm yet fair.

AVOID THESE PITFALLS

- favoritism
- not following through
- forgetting what you said
- not rewarding good behavior

Discipline (or a discipline plan) is a guide . . . a guide you use to move a group of students from point A to point B, or from day 1 to the final bell, so that you can accomplish the goals set down for that year.

Always discipline children as though their parents are in the room. Always give the student a chance to explain and change. Please be clear on why the behavior they exhibited is unacceptable. If the behavior persists, then inform them that you need to talk to them after school.

Don't ever make fun of any student.

Under no circumstance is it ever OK to make fun of a student. It doesn't matter if you're mad or just playing around or if the student has just made fun of you. Remember, you're the adult and the leader, and they're children and they're vulnerable.
No cheap shots. Effective teachers would never tolerate using humiliation and ridicule on anyone, let alone their own students.

Your most challenging student, the one who tries your patience most often, could become (and many times does) your favorite student by the end of the year.

Humor is acceptable; ridicule is not.

HUMOR	HUMILIATION
healthy	unhealthy
acceptable	unacceptable
reduces stress	creates stress
produces laughter	produces sadness
can create closeness	will create distance

Q "It's nice to be important, but it's more important to be nice." *-John Cassis*

NOTES

1984

"A dinner party for 35? No problem... I'm cookin'!"

⑩ Be Organized

We've all heard that organization is the key to
success, and most who are successful would agree.
Nowhere does this advice prove more necessary
than in the classroom. Teachers are required to be
multi-tasked individuals; people who can execute
and manage many tasks at one time. In order to
manage many tasks at one time, an individual
must be organized.

Whether you were just hired or you've been teaching ten years, an effective teacher needs to be organized. Being organized means having:

1. a plan.

2. a system for implementing the plan.

3. a method that can be used for evaluating the plan.

4. a commitment to change the plan if it's not working.

Regardless of the activity. . .

- students entering your classroom

- holding a class discussion

- collecting homework

- ordering supplies, etc.

. . . being organized is vital if you want to build and maintain a successful A+ classroom.

Think of your classroom as a small business, and you're the executive director. Your stockholders (*the parents*) and the Board of Directors (*the school district*) expect you to show a profit. The ones who will profit the most are your students.

1. Order supplies before you need them.

Every school has a procedure or system for ordering classroom supplies. Most often it requires your name, your school, your room number, and you checking off items you need from a preprinted catalog. Unfortunately, schools and school districts vary on the time frame as to when you'll actually receive those supplies in your classroom. In fact, many schools/school districts have switched to the system where you buy the materials you need, then you submit the receipts to the office, and they reimburse you.

However, a good rule of thumb says submit your order 3-4 weeks ahead of when you plan on needing certain specific materials. Also, know what your yearly classroom budget is, and don't waste money on unneeded supplies. Don't spend all your money on one big project and have nothing for the rest of the year. Run your classroom like a small business . . budgeting your finances is important.

2. Before your students enter the classroom, have the agenda on the board and all the materials you'll need for that class or lesson ready to go.

Don't waste valuable class time. Be organized by planning ahead.

3. Have substitute plans
(There's no substitute for good plans.)

It doesn't matter how organized you are, the best laid plans can change. You wake up one morning and realize you or your child has the flu, or suddenly one afternoon your principal states that you would be perfect for the conference scheduled tomorrow morning, or, more often the case, you have car trouble, and now you have to leave lesson plans.

My advice is simple: plan for the unexpected. Prepare a substitute folder ahead of time and include the following:

• A seating chart for the class or classes you teach.

• A lesson plan for each subject or class you teach.

• An easy-to-follow lesson or activity that includes ample work for the entire period.

• The number to the office and the number to your buddy teacher in the event the sub has a question or problem.

• Names of students that can always be counted on for support and honest answers.

• Names of students the sub needs to keep an eye on.

Tell your students what you expect from them on days when you have a substitute:

• behave as though I was in the classroom

• treat the sub with respect

• let them know that you will be checking with the sub as to how the class behaved

Praise your class or classes for behaving appropriately.

An organized teacher:

• is always prepared

• teaches the students the classroom rules and procedures

• has a discipline plan

• teaches the students where to locate books and materials

• has a seating chart

• doesn't waste valuable class time.

Q "Leave as little to chance as possible. Preparation is the key to success."

-Paul Brown

NOTES

Posing with future stars only days away from opening night.

⑪ Get to Know Your Audience

Your audience is your students. You're probably going to be together for many months. You've carefully designed dynamic lessons that when presented will transform your students into self-driven, goal-oriented caring productive individuals, who because of what you've instilled in them, send you bags of money each month as a small way of saying, "Thanks – you helped me a lot." Naturally, it's good to have goals, and maybe, when Peter Pan returns one day, this scenario will one day actually come true.

In the meantime, I suggest that if you hope to reach your students *QUICKER*, *SOONER*, *FASTER*, that you spend a little time getting to really know them.

ASK AND YOU SHALL RECEIVE

I'm glad you asked. Here are some techniques, t
and activities that helped me reach my student

Quicker   Sooner   Faster.

(*These are not in any divine order.*)

1. Have them complete a personal invento
   (*Because I kept a file on each student, an 8 1/2 x 11 s
   worked best for me. Index cards work great, also.*)

Include:
   • Parents' names (*first and last*).
   Many students have a different last name
   than their parents

   • Siblings' names and ages

   • Home phone number

   • Mom and Dad's work number or cell numbe

I only wanted info. about family members who lived with them each day.

2. Find out which activities your students enjoy doing when they're not in class.

Most students have a hobby or pastime (*maybe more than one*) they love doing when they're not in class. Maybe they love playing video games or listening to music or reading or playing basketball. The list is endless. By finding out what they enjoy doing you come that much closer to understanding who they are. The more you know about your students, the easier it becomes when you're trying to reach and teach them.

TRY THIS!

• Occasionally use part of your lunch break to walk around and see where your students eat and hang out.

• At the beginning of the year have your students fill out a survey entitled, FAVORITES. It's fun for them to do, it's fun for you to read, and, more importantly, you get immediate feedback about what they like and the fads they follow.

(EXAMPLE)

Favorites

food	hobby
movie star	ice cream
soft drink	grade in school
music performer	candy
restaurant	video or computer
amusement park	game
color	magazine
vacation spot	subject in school
TV program	book
radio station	TV star
movie	sport
place to hang out	day of the week
music	number

3. Have them write a story entitled, "Me, Myself, and I."

It should be fairly informal, but you might want to lead them in the direction of including their physical characteristics (*i.e. color of hair, color of eyes, height, etc.*), their accomplishments, their disappointments, their dreams, and their fears.

Q "Minds, like parachutes, only work when they are open."

-Author Unkn

⑫ The Unmatch Game

It's the beginning of the year, or it's the beginning of a lesson or activity that you hope will inspire and teach the anticipated outcome of a unit you have diligently prepared for many days. You know the standard and you have done your homework, yet there are times when you feel like you're not connecting . . . like you're not in sync with the particular class you're teaching.

I know the feeling. I would spend endless hours preparing material, anticipating problems, designing solutions, creating plan B's and C's, and yet I found I wasn't connecting or "matching up" with a particular class. A good teacher knows that the more they know about their students and how they behave in certain situations, the easier and faster they will be able to teach and inspire their students. Every class is different because every class has a personality. Understanding the students, their personalities and their specific behavior in a given situation allows the teacher to better teach a lesson or concept *QUICKER*, *SOONER*, *FASTER*. In other words, the faster you get to know your students and the way they learn and interact in the learning process, the more successful you'll be in providing them a positive link or "match" to the skills you know they need.

This is the reason why I created "The Unmatch Game". I wanted one more way to better understand my students.

Society is comprised of individuals, each unique and wonderful . . . the unmatches. As a teacher, you have the unique opportunity to reach individuals and match or share their special talents and contributions with one another.

Here's How to Play

This is a great game because the whole class gets to participate. It's best played if you have your students sitting in rows.

O	O	O	O	O	O
O	O	O	O	O	O
O	O	O	O	O	O
O	O	O	O	O	O
O	O	O	O	O	O
O	O	O	O	O	O
Team 2	Team 1	Team 2	Team 1	Team 2	Team 1

Every other row is on the same team. Students are not allowed to talk, look sideways, or turn around. I always told them that this game is fun and exciting, and you'll learn some new facts today. However, it's mainly about trust. Once you write an answer down, you cannot change it. If anyone is caught changing an answer, then his/her team forfeits that round and loses any points they may have received. Also, if any student gives an answer that's different than the one he/she has written on their paper, then that also constitutes a forfeit and loss of points for their team.

Let's Get Started

First, I would announce a category, such as colors. (*I've provided a pretty extensive list at the end of this chapter*), and each student from both teams would write down a color.

Next, I would tell them to put all pens and pencils down. Anyone caught holding a pen or pencil during the first round automatically disqualifies their team and a chance to get points.

Then, starting with Team 1 (*remind Team 2 that they're not playing right now*) each student gives their answer out loud. If no other student on Team 1 raises their hand as a match, then a point is given to Team 1. Hence the title, "The Unmatch Game."

(*Note: If a student has already matched with another, then that student should say, "Pass" when it comes to their turn.*)

After completing Team 1, follow the same procedure for Team 2. Remind them that they're only competing against their own team. Remember, unmatches score a point. The team with the most points wins that round.

Finally, depending on your time limit, you can do several rounds before declaring a winner.

(*Note: Never start a round if you don't think you have enough time to complete it.*)

THE "UNMATCH GAME" IS A GREAT GAME BECAUSE:

• students learn facts and information

• students work as a team

• all students in class get to participate

• it's fun to play

Categories

road signs	grocery store chains	appliances
subjects in school	fast food chains	plants
gas stations	planets	cereals
board games	sports	desserts
game shows	states	disasters
trees	colors	U.S. Presidents
flowers	magazines	countries
types of music	parts of a car	famous battles
religions	zodiac signs	math terms
car manufacturers	fruit	elements
articles of clothing	meat	historical events
vegetables	track events	famous people
dairy products	bodies of water	
soft drinks	olympic events	
candy bars	tv stations	
restaurants	birds	

"It's not always elementary, my dear Watson."

(13) Keep a File For Each Student

This is not to be confused with a portfolio, and it's also not something you would write in on a daily or even weekly basis. This folder is a place where you can note observations or accomplishments or concerns about any student at any given time.

FOR INSTANCE, ONE OF YOUR STUDENTS:

- was chosen Student of the Month

- had perfect attendance last trimester

- got into a fight after school

- has begun raising her hand and actively participating more

- wrote an incredible essay in history

- is dealing with his parents' divorce

- is missing three homework assignments

- often has to be reminded to stop talking

- has a learning disability

Everything you note or write down will ultimately help you understand your students

Quicker Sooner Faster.

BONUS

You'll be attending hundreds of parent conferences during your career. I suggest you review the student's file before the conference. If it doesn't contain confidential information, then you might want to bring it to the conference along with your grade book and the student's portfolio.

⑭ Put The Homework On the Board

Put the homework on the board (*or overhead or screen*) and make sure they copy it in their folders or in their planners.*

Whether you have the homework for the day on the board when the students enter the classroom, or you write it on the board at the end of the period, make sure you leave time for each student to write the homework assignments in their planner. Continually stress the importance of writing down their homework in their planner and periodically check to ensure this is happening.

At the beginning of the year for the first two weeks, make sure you check their planners each day. This ensures that your students will continue the practice of recording their assignments throughout the year. Choose a different day each week from then on to randomly check their planners.

* A planner is an organizer which includes a calendar to record homework and dates when projects are due. It often includes a pocket or slot for papers that need to go home for parents to review.

Flash!

It's also a good idea to have their parents initial their planners every Thursday evening, and you check their planners every Friday. It only takes a few minutes. This can be done during a pop quiz or test, or even while they're working on an assignment or worksheet.

HAVING THE PARENTS INITIAL THE PLANNERS ACCOMPLISHES TWO THINGS:

☐ 1. it's another form of communication between you and the parent

☐ 2. it gives the parent a quick reminder of what has been the focus for that week

(15) Homework Competition

I created HOMEWORK COMPETITION in 1985.
I started to notice some reluctance in students to
have their homework completed on time, and I also
started to see a decline in parental control and
involvement. I don't believe in rewarding students
for every little thing they do, especially when it
involves completing required tasks and acting
responsibly. Did I make a big deal every day about
working hard? Yes. Did I encourage them to
strive harder and noticed when they did? Yes.
Did I prepare for class every day and, therefore,
presented myself as a successful, healthy role
model? Yes.

However, as a dedicated, caring leader I saw what
I observed as complacency toward commitment.
It's true they enjoyed my class and respected me
as their teacher, yet I wanted every student to
experience success, push themselves a little
harder, and ultimately feel in their hearts that
they are truly being prepared for the challenges
that await them in the future.

There's no reason why working toward a common
goal can't be fun and exciting. Hence, I created
HOMEWORK COMPETITION as a vehicle large
enough to carry everyone. Getting my students to
complete their homework on time and also to know
why this behavior was important became my goal.

THE RULES:

- If every student in the class or period had their homework completed on time, then that class or period received one homework point. (*I included daily assignments, as well as projects, reports, and presentations that might require more time to prepare.*)

- I did not penalize a class or period if a student or students were absent on the day something was due.

- The class or period that got the most A's on a test or quiz also received a point in the competition.

- If I was absent on a day when an assignment was due, then I left explicit instructions for the sub to let me know which class or classes completed their work on time.

THE BENEFITS:

- The students work as a team.

- The students learn the benefits of everyone doing their part.

- Homework gets completed on time.

- The winning class or period gets a pizza party after the trimester ends.

- The students learn delayed gratification.

- Substitutes can collect homework and projects without a glitch.

Also, I awarded a special point to the best behaved class.

I always provided the substitute with an easy-to-use rating scale to determine the most well behaved class for that day.

As you can imagine, classes very quickly figured out that working together and supporting one another got them a point. But as the year progressed, most students figured out the "point" or benefits of the competition, and carried this discipline with them into their other academic classes. It became a win-win situation.

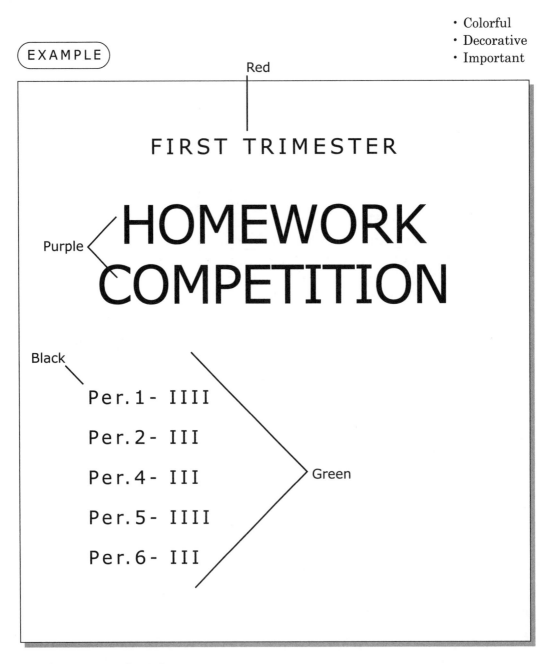

- Colorful
- Decorative
- Important

EXAMPLE

Red

FIRST TRIMESTER

HOMEWORK
COMPETITION

Purple

Black

Per. 1 - IIII

Per. 2 - III

Per. 4 - III

Green

Per. 5 - IIII

Per. 6 - III

Use large posterboard.

Alternate colors for effect.

1979

"Spell the word _awesome_."

(16) Keep Students Informed of How They're Doing in Your Class

Students want to know how they're doing in your class. They may not act like they do, but the majority really want an update on their progress. It doesn't matter whether they're self-motivated, they've turned a corner and are working hard to improve, or they know if they don't do well they'll be put on restriction for life. Regardless of the impetus, students deserve a periodic heads-up on how they're progressing in your class.

It's true most districts and schools send home a progress report midway through the quarter or trimester. It's been my experience that this is not enough. I wanted my students to stay current as to progress, improvement, and meeting expectations, and at the same time, keep their desire to do their best at its optimum. So, along with rallying the troops to keep moving forward, I provided my students with a variety of indicators of how they were doing.

HERE ARE SOME ASSESSMENT TOOLS THAT WORK:

- pop quizzes

- announced quizzes

- tests

- projects

- presentations

- homework

- classwork

- notes

- behavior checklist

1985

Teaching is a moving experience.

(17) Leave a Few Minutes at the End of Each Class Period or Activity for Questions, Transition, and Clean-up

Discounting the days when you are "in the groove" and suddenly the bell rings, try to leave two or three minutes at the end of each period, class, or activity for closure. This gives you the opportunity to change gears, answer questions, give a homework reminder, and move to the door to say goodbye. It also allows students to change gears. Remember, no matter how incredibly awesome or inspiring your class my have been, your students still have to refocus for their next class, get into a different mind set for a big test they're about to take in the next class, say hi to their best friend, go to the bathroom or get a drink, and make it to the next class period on time.

Let's be realistic. If you haven't reached them by the last two or three minutes of the class, you're probably not going to reach them that day. Besides, some students might have questions or concerns and they're not going to share them if they think they're going to be late to their next class.

So, leave a few minutes at the end of the period or activity, and eliminate the stress for everyone.

Thought For The Day

GREAT IDEA!

At the end of every class or activity, provide time for cleaning up. Students need to learn the importance of keeping their area or work station clean. It shows ownership, and, at the same time, encourages respect for other people.

BONUS

Your room will be clean and ready for the next class or activity.

Challenge your students to be leaders, not followers.

⑱ Be Professional

Regardless of the career you choose, the number one requirement for you to achieve success in that career is to always be professional. I cannot emphasize this tip enough. Remember, you're a teacher, a role model, a professional . . . and what you say and what you do have, a profound impact on the young people you teach. So imagine again that you're the CEO and every day you enter your classroom to teach you're setting the tone, influencing others, and making a difference in hundreds of students' lives. Have fun, but please take it seriously.

1) Be on time to school.

Most schools, because of contractual agreements with their local union, require you to be on campus before school begins and after school ends a said amount of minutes.

My advice to you is always arrive at school at least 30 minutes before your first class begins. This gives you ample time to visualize your lesson, put notes or diagrams on the board, make sure your room is ready to go, check in the office and retrieve your mail from your teacher's box, and check your emails.

You can't expect your students to be punctual if you're not. Effective teachers arrive on time and are ready and prepared to meet their students at the door when the bell rings.

TIPS FOR THE PROFESSIONAL

• Never use bad language or vulgarity in the classroom.

• Never lose your temper (*or your cool*).

• Never use class time to talk about your personal problems.

• If you want respect, then show respect.

If, for some unforeseen circumstance (*i.e. your child is ill, you're caught in a traffic jam, you're involved in a traffic accident, etc.*) you find you're running late, then call the school and let them know you're running late. Unexpected emergencies can happen to anyone. This allows the school to get another teacher/administrator to cover your class until you arrive. It also shows your superiors that you were responsible enough to call in.

SUGGESTIONS

- Don't be late.

- If you think you might be late, call the school.

- Make sure you thank the individual who covered your class.*

> *Pay them back by covering one of their classes one day, or take them out to lunch, or buy them a gift.   The point is, don't let it go unnoticed.

2) Don't leave school early.

When I say leaving school early, I mean leaving the school grounds before you're contractually allowed to leave. If you plan on being employed next year, then don't leave early. Besides, many students only have time at the end of the school day to come by your classroom and ask for additional help, ask a question about your homework assignment, or talk to you about a problem.

Barring a staff meeting or an occasional parent conference, effective teachers always remain in their classrooms long after the final bell has rung. Whether it's to counsel a student, offer some additional help to students who need further clarification, or prepare materials for the next day, effective teachers aren't seen leaving campus the second they can. Make it a point to stay longer than required, and you'll be surprised at the benefits of this decision.

EXCEPTIONS TO THE RULE:

- You have a sick child at home.

- You have a doctor's appointment.

- You have to attend another meeting off campus.

- You have an appointment that's important.

These are exceptions, and if not abused, will most always be cleared by your administrator.

3) Never leave your classroom unattended.

I cannot stress this rule enough. Remember, you are responsible (and therefore liable) for every student registered in your class or particular period, and that definitely includes their safety and well-being. So, unless it's an emergency, don't ever leave your classroom with students in attendance. Planning for an emergency or unforeseen problem is a priority for all effective teachers. You might suddenly become ill, or you receive a phone call from your child's school that he/she is ill, or a fight breaks out between two students in front of your door . . . whatever the emergency might be, always try to do the following:

1) Call the office and inform them of the problem. That way they can send someone down immediately to cover your class.

2) Alert the teachers on either side of you that you are going to be away from your classroom and why.

3) Never leave your classroom unattended unless it's an absolute emergency.

Q "Teaching is the profession that teaches all other professions." *-Author Unknown*

NOTES

Parents get a 'thumbs up' for attending Back to School Night.

⑲ Communicate with Parents

When communicating with parents, whether it be via phone, parent conference, or note home, always be positive, professional, and succinct. Do not rant, rave, or ramble. Parents for the most part appreciate a heads up if there's a problem, so they can help eliminate it early.

If a parent were to become hostile or uncooperative, then you simply conclude the dialogue cordially and turn the problem over to administration. It is not in your job description to take verbal abuse from anyone.

And now on a lighter note. . .

Don't forget to call home or send a note home when a student has done something terrific, or aced a big test, or has really improved since the last communiqué. All parents like to hear that their child is doing great in school.

Keep a parent contact/phone log.

It's always good business to keep a record of all contacts you have with your students' parents. Parents will occasionally call with questions or concerns or information about their child, and I strongly recommend that you document these communications.

Remember, for the most part, parents only know what their child shares with them when they get home at the end of the day. Most students give an accurate account of their day's activities, have their homework assignments legibly written down in their planner, and give their parents all communiqués sent home that day. However, you will have a few students who, when asked to describe their day, will distort particular incidences that happened that day, who will invariably forget to write down a couple of homework assignments, and who will either deny receiving a notice that was to go home or more often, can't remember what they did with it.

In any case, jot down a few notes from any conversation you've had with any of your students' parents.

FLASH!! *Read all about it!*

Everything you say and do goes home . . . as it should.

Often times a parent who is enabling his/her child will state in a parent conference that they were never notified of a particular problem or situation. You have the log to repudiate that accusation. It also shows that you care about their child and that you, in fact, did contact them concerning the particular problem or situation.

PARENT CONTACT/PHONE LOG

Student's name	Phone #	Contact Person	Date	Reason for calling

FOR YOUR EYES ONLY

This is confidential information. Therefore, it should never be left out for other students or staff to see.

NOTES

Don't be square ... dance!

⑳ Visit Other Classrooms

I'm pretty sure you've heard the phrase
"reinvent the wheel", and probably in the
context of why would you. Exactly. So why not
learn some tricks and effective techniques early,
and maybe eliminate making some unnecessary
rookie mistakes.

If you are fortunate enough to have a planning
period, then I suggest you take one day a week and
visit classrooms where effective teaching is taking
place. Make sure you contact the teacher you'd
like to visit ahead of time and together you both
can coordinate the best day. Make the effort to
visit as many of these classrooms as you can.
The more you visit, the more you learn.

Many schools have mentor teacher programs in place and often the teacher is provided a sub so that he/she can visit specific master teachers and observe how they handle everyday procedures and situations such as classroom management, time on task, student involvement, and administering tests.

It really boils down to you ultimately finding and using what works for you, thereby enhancing your chances of reaching your students

Quicker   Sooner   Faster.

Remember, this book demonstrates my way, but it's not the only way. You need to find your way . . . your style.

BONUS

If any educator tells you their way is the only way, then you need to run away.

1976

Some staff meetings can get pretty crazy.

㉑ Work With Your Staff

You've just been hired and you have a million things racing through your head. You've prepared and planned and somehow got yourself ready for your new assignment. Or, you've taught for many years and you have made preparations for the new school year. Regardless of your tenure, CONGRATULATIONS! Now, get to know your colleagues. These are individuals who, like you, love teaching and working with students. They really would like to know you and share their hundreds of stories about reaching students with you.

Take the time to listen, and you'll probably pick up some tips from the voices of experience. There's no reward for reinventing the wheel, especially one that keeps turning out successful, happy students. Learn from the masters, and they, in turn, will learn from you. Remember, treat people the way you would like to be treated.

TIPS

- Ask a veteran teacher for advice.

- Ask a veteran teacher to be your mentor.

- Make your staff members your allies.

- Get to know the school's secretary and custodian.

- Keep an open mind.

- Don't leave your sense of humor at home.

Q "Kindness adds and multiplies when you divide it with others."

-Author Unknown

Extracurricular activities give students the opportunity to feel like royalty.

(22) Take Part in Activities Sponsored by the School and Encourage Students to Do the Same

I'm sure you've heard the phrase, "Be a team player," and I'm also sure you've observed or experienced the benefits of what that phrase implicates. In the school setting it doesn't mean compromising your personal goals or having to support a business plan you believe to be unethical.

On the contrary, taking part in school sponsored activities reinforces the notion that you're involved in something very meaningful. Students learn from what the teacher says and from what the teacher does. I guarantee they'll remember what the teacher does a lot longer.

Taking part in activities outside the classroom tells most students that you are a "fun" person, that you like your job and this school, and that you like kids. You'll be surprised at how fast this extra involvement carries over into the classroom in the form of commitment and respect.

It also encourages students to take some healthy risks and to try something new. They learn through example. They see you involved and it looks like fun, so they often give it a try.

As an activities director for over 20 years, I was constantly creating new activities and opportunities for more students to be involved. There is a direct correlation between an exciting well-managed extracurricular program and a reduction in school-wide absenteeism. You can't teach them if they're not in school.

Below is a list of some of the activities I created or
helped sponsor during my 30-year tenure:

School-wide Speech Tournament

School-wide Spelling Bee

Best Friends Game Show

Scholastic Roundup

Trivimania

Noon-time sports program

School-wide track and field competition

After-school dances

Competitive contests during lunch

Career Day

Student Council

Drama Club

Homework Club

Comic Book Club

Yearbook

Field Day

Medieval Day

Maybe one of these would work for you.

Q "Be yourself. An original is worth more than a copy."
-Author Unknown

NOTES

1986

"What did your best friend say was *your* favorite sport?"

(23) The Best Friends Game Show

Many years ago I wanted to design an activity that fostered friendship. Having good friends is truly a blessing. A bad day can become a good day, or at least more tolerable, if you have a good friend. Close friends help us enjoy life more, and often their influence helps us make better decisions and healthier choices.

So based on the 70's TV game show, "The Newlywed Game," I created and hosted "The Best Friends Game." For three or four days during lunch, pairs of best friends would come to my room and audition for the show. A couple of my best friends and myself would ask three or four questions to each couple. We used two criteria to guide our questioning: 1) were these two students truly best friends, and 2) could these two friends handle the pressure of being on stage answering funny, ridiculous questions in front of the entire eighth grade?

Because of space constraints on stage, I found six pairs of friends worked best visually. I arranged the twelve chairs in a semi-circle facing the audience, and the host (*that's me*) would be at a podium positioned stage right.

After I welcomed the audience and explained the rules and purpose of the game, I had one friend for each pair (*usually the one on the right*) escorted to a soundproof room (*the office*) and began the game. The remaining six friends on stage would each be asked ten questions and their responses would be recorded. My six recorders sat at a table in front of the stage and each was responsible for recording the answers of one of the pairs of best friends. Once all responses were recorded, we brought back the students from the "soundproof booth" and asked them the same ten questions. If the answer matched what had been recorded, that pair received ten points and a bell went off. If the answers did not match, then a horn went off denoting zero points and they were free to argue, act silly, and entertain the audience.

The second half of the show is run the same as the first half (*different questions of course*) except, after the tenth question I would ask a bonus question worth 25 points. Those of you who remember "The Newlywed Game" know how critical the bonus question was . . it could change everything.

Well, needless to say, the pair that had the most points at the end of the game was the winner. They were afforded many honors, such as:

• receiving a plaque

• having their picture taken for the yearbook

• being featured in the school newspaper

• being honored at the next School Board Meeting

Having good friends and choosing friends that care about you was very much supported at the school in which I taught. Every student at your school is important, and needs to feel important. This activity is just one of many ways that as a class or as a school you can provide ways for students to link to you and link to teaming. Every time a student hurts himself or hurts other students, we all lose.

NOTES

"Don't be shy. Step right up and win yourself a medal."

㉔ The Voice of Rogers

I'm a firm believer in the adage, "The more you give, the more you get." I tried to give more than 100% each day as a teacher, mentor, and activities director, and for me the payoff was remarkable.

Students are very quick to pick up on which teachers go the extra mile, stay a little later, and are responsible for orchestrating a special event or activity. In short, these are the teachers who manage to muster just a little more energy for an activity or event above and beyond their job description.

As activities director I placed myself on stage as much as I could. Consequently, students got used to seeing me and hearing my voice. I enjoyed this forum a lot because I could reach more students

Quicker   *Sooner*   *Faster*

and still have fun.

Also, I had the distinct honor of literally being the "Voice of Rogers" because each morning during homeroom for about ten years I read the announcements over the PA system. I viewed it more as a show than a reading. As it turned out, my voice became something students looked forward to hearing each day.

I was a "voice" at Rogers because I wanted to be more involved. As a a result, I got to know more students and they got to see another side of me. This translated into stronger, healthier relationships with my students, a reduction in the number and types of classroom discipline problems, and a greater respect for me as a role model.

25 Never Make a Decision When You're Angry

I don't care whether you're having the worst day of your life or the principal just chewed you out or Bobby just told you where you might want to stick your predicate nominative, this is a child and you're the adult. I didn't say you can't get mad . . . you can. What I am definitely pointing out is the fact that no constructive decision or learning ever resulted from an angry overreaction.

Follow your discipline plan, assign the consequence, diffuse the problem or hostility, and move on. Maintain your professionalism and never lose your cool. Remember, it's drama, Mama! Nine times out of ten the student is dealing with another issue or is having a bad day. Regardless, don't internalize unnecessary stress and get on with the business of teaching. Of course, if the problem child persists with his/her need for negative attention, call the office and have the student removed.

Once the problem is solved or removed, resume teaching as though nothing happened.

Q "Anger is only one letter short of danger."
-Author Unknown

NOTES

1982

I tried to go for the home run with every student.

㉖ Encourage Students to Care About Others

The minute I had my students enter the classroom and find their seats, I began my "sales pitch" about caring for others. It was very important to me that every student felt welcome and safe and ready to learn. As they entered my class the first day, I greeted them at the door with phrases like:

"Good morning, good to see you!"

"How ya' doing . . . find your seat."

"Everybody wins . . . because you're in my class."

"Excuse me! Did I hear someone say, 'This is a great class?'"

"Everybody gets a seat . . . we turn no one away."

If you build it, they will come.

I explained to my students on Day 1 that everyone in my class is very important, just as important as me. So, we all need to help one another to learn and to grow and to be happy.

I would say to my students at the beginning of each new school year, "Let's get started today. Nine months is barely enough time to get to really know you, let alone enough time to teach you and inspire you. I'm thrilled to be your teacher and you're lucky to be my students. I only have nine months to prepare you for the future . . . but right now, I know more than you. Therefore, you must trust me. . . but trust doesn't happen overnight. So you must watch, listen and learn, and I guarantee that in a very short period of time you'll love learning as much as I do, and you'll be more successful than you've ever been before. Oh, and by the way, if you ever have something bothering you that's keeping you from being a success story in my class, I'm always available to listen. Now, take out a pen and a piece of paper. We've got some dancin' to do!

Q "A good teacher is one who loves to teach so others will love to learn." *-Author Unknown*

NOTES

(27) The Giving Tree

Like any good teacher I was always trying to provide positive experiences within the classroom that demonstrated or reinforced the importance of caring for others, especially those less fortunate than ourselves. I wanted to replace the crutches and the excuses which support a "feel sorry for me" attitude, and replace them with better social skills and a higher regard for others.

For most of my career I taught in a very wonderful community. However, many of our families struggled with divorce, unemployment, alcoholism, drug abuse, gang activity, and low self-esteem. Suffice it to say, Christmas was not always the huge holiday it had been when I was growing up. So one December I bought a Christmas tree and some decorations, and told my classes that we'd have a little holiday celebration on the last day before vacation. I told them I would provide some treats and we'd play some games. They thought that was a pretty cool idea.

I happened to mention to my classes that wouldn't it be great if the tree and all the decorations could go to a family that maybe was struggling this time of year. They agreed. I told them to tell their parents about our idea and maybe they could contact their local churches and find a needy family.

The response was overwhelming and I was overwhelmed. I only had one tree. A minister called me that same afternoon, told me he had the perfect family for our special gift (*a large family . . . two adults – both unemployed, and six children ranging in age from one to fourteen*), and said he would provide transportation for the tree. My students and I were thrilled and they asked if I knew the ages and genders of the children. I provided that information, and the next day, they brought in food and clothes and toys for the family. I was very proud of them, and they were very proud of themselves.

On Friday afternoon around 4:00 p.m. the minister, his assistant, and the family's mother arrived to pick up the tree. About 40 students stayed after school to help and to also meet the family. The mother was crying and smiling, and the minister was speechless. Many of my students were also crying. Along with the tree, we gave them 12 bags of groceries and 20 boxes of clothes and toys that my students had donated that week. I took lots of pictures and shared them with my classes when they returned from winter break.

For the 40 or so students that stayed after school that day it was a memory that each of them will share with others many times during their lifetime. For the next 20 years I got to experience this incredible gift every December.

With the right encouragement from me, my students managed each year to find the perfect family for our "Giving Tree."

2003

Always try to put yourself on the winning team.

㉘ Be Available

One of my top goals as a teacher for over 30 years was
to reach my students any way I could. If it meant I
could help a student succeed and enjoy learning more,
then I went the extra mile. So I made it my business
to be in my classroom with the door open before the
gates opened in the morning. If I needed to see a
student and that student couldn't get to school early,
then I remained in my classroom after the lunch bell
rang. I always stayed after school (*unless I had a staff
meeting*) to meet and work with students who needed
additional help, or who maybe had a question about
the lesson or homework, or who maybe had a personal

concern and didn't feel comfortable talking with me during the day. Regardless of the reason, an effective teacher makes him or herself available so that any student who needs help gets that help. Remember, the more you give, the more you learn about your students. The more you know about your students, the QUICKER, SOONER, FASTER you can help them become informed, productive citizens and happy successful people.

It's a WIN-WIN situation.

Q "To the world, you may be one person; but to one person, you may be the world." *-Author Unknown*

㉙ Brown Bag It

The more you know about the students you teach, the better year you'll have and the fewer discipline problems you'll have to encounter.

Lunch time for most students, and most teachers, is a time to relax, take a break from the normal routine of school, and hang out with friends. I, on the other hand, saw this time as an opportunity to plan, design, or set up the next activity or fund raiser for that week. Because of necessity (*completely brought on by me*), I stayed in my room two or three days a week during lunch. For those familiar with working through lunch, I "brown bagged it."

This was very early in my career, maybe my fifth or sixth year teaching. A very dear friend at the time encouraged me to take on challenges beyond the classroom. He successfully produced and hosted the annual Speech Tournament, which at the time was one of the premiere activities of the year and he allowed me to play a small part. It didn't take long before I understood the benefits of extracurricular activities and spawned the annual Spelling Bee. This was the first of hundreds of activities that I created and implemented during my tenure as activities director.

Most students crave and will seek out additional ways to not only shine and find acceptance, but also benefit from programs which give them the opportunity to be more closely linked to their school. The solution to apathy is spirit.

But I digress. The point I'm making is it might very well benefit you to "brown bag it" one day each week and meet a few more students who otherwise you wouldn't really get to know. Or, maybe you just want to get caught up so you can stay on top of your goals that week. Regardless of the reason, I found it very beneficial to "brown bag it" at least one day each week.

1978

These students chose to be successful.

(30) Give Your Students Choices

We cannot expect students to make good responsible choices if we don't give them opportunities to make good choices. This requires us, as teachers, to occasionally step back, and allow them to make some on their own. This doesn't mean you sit back and allow your students to decide how your class will be organized or what lesson they'd like to learn. That's not realistic and it's definitely not in line with effective teaching.

However, what you can do is allow them to periodically have input into a particular activity or pre-planned lesson. This affords your students opportunities to demonstrate good decision making.

(EXAMPLES)

- If you're teaching the elements of a story and you have several good short stories you like to use, then read the titles and let the class decide which one they'd like to do first.

- Whenever I assigned the class a project, report, speech or presentation, I did one also. If it required presenting the assignment in front of the class, I always asked them, "Would someone like to volunteer to go first, or would you like me to go first?"

TRY THIS!

Throughout the school year provide your students with lots of opportunities to be leaders.

Q "A successful person has failed many more times than an unsuccessful person." *-Author Unknown*

㉛ Fantasy Weekend

Imagine this scenario: You've won . . that's right, you've won an all expenses paid vacation for you and your best friend. What does that mean, you ask? You and your friend can go anywhere you want, all expenses paid, to any fantasy vacation resort or resorts you want. We, Fantasy Vacations Come True, will fly you and your lucky friend to any paradise you desire and pay for all the activities and meals you can pack into one incredible weekend. Did I hear someone say, "It's too wonderful to believe?" Well, it's true! One person in each class will be chosen to have their dream come true.

But, as with any contest, there are rules, and these rules must be followed precisely. Not following these rules could result in disqualification of desired dream. Before I list these nagging rules, let me remind you that this activity is a wonderful opportunity for you to explore new worlds, use your imagination and creativity, and hopefully inspire you to always follow your dreams.

I created this activity because I wanted to encourage my students to dream. And even though this activity is just for fun and not a reality now, I planted an idea in their heads that said, "Who knows, maybe one day through hard work and determination, this fantasy weekend (*or any other goal*) could become a dream come true for me."

Fantasy Weekend Rules:

1) All flights leave at 4 p.m. on Friday, and must return at midnight on Sunday.

2) Your project must include the following:
   - a colorful cover
   - a business letter
   - a Time Schedule
   - an Expense Account

3) If time permits, you may travel to more than one destination.

4) In place of a friend, you can take a family member.

5) Excluding the cover, the project must be typed.

6) Do a one-minute oral presentation to the class about your project.

Naturally I went over each rule in detail with each class. The excitement and enthusiasm were always overwhelming. I usually introduced this project right after I taught my classes how to write a business letter and how to conduct an interview.

Throughout this project my students were exposed to
the following concepts, skills, and experiences:

- following directions

- meeting deadlines

- the business letter

- planning an itinerary

- estimating cost

- making choices

- time zones

- geography

- taking notes

- cooperative learning

- setting goals

- layout design

- public speaking

- conducting research

NOTES

1989

"Ladies and gentlemen, may I have your attention please."

㉜ Teach Your Students to Listen When Someone Else is Speaking

Aside from the fact that it's just common courtesy not to talk when someone else is speaking, it demonstrates to your class that each person's views are both valued and valuable. I recommend you reinforce this skill at the beginning of the year or the start of a new class. Again, it sets the tone for the direction you want your class to head, and it provides a forum which supports respect for another person's opinion.

Listen to these:

- Require your students to raise their hand before asking or answering questions.

- Never allow your students to blurt out answers. Some students (*and adults*) need a few more seconds to process the information and arrive at an answer.

- Be an active listener yourself. Refrain from interrupting or cutting off your students because you think you know what they're about to say. Let them finish.

- During an oral presentation (*i.e. book talk, giving a speech, visitor speaker, you, etc.*), no one in the class should be speaking except the individual on stage.

> **TIP**
>
> Occasionally call on students who never raise their hands. It gives those students who might be shy or more reluctant to participate a chance to shine and feel successful. Many students know the answers; they're just less confident in a group setting.
>
> The reason I said occasionally is because some students become embarrassed easily. All you want to do is boost their self-confidence in a very safe setting.

Q "We have two ears and one mouth for a reason." *-Author Unknown*

NOTES

For me, teaching meant I'd died and gone to heaven.

㉝ Don't Be Afraid To Make A Mistake

Many people are too hard on themselves when they make a mistake. They're generally concerned more with image or with looking foolish in front of their peers, rather than with learning from the mistake and improving their lives. How else can we learn and change and grow if we don't recognize that making mistakes is an integral part of the learning curve.

Curtis Zimmerman, inspirational speaker, author, friend, and former student calls this "failing successfully." The average person tries less than ten times at learning something new before completely giving up and never trying again. Curtis says, "Give yourself 5000 tries and you might be amazed at what you <u>can</u> do."

As any effective teacher will tell you, in order for students to learn, the teacher must provide a healthy, safe environment where asking questions, taking risks, and learning from mistakes is par for the course. I always told my students repeatedly throughout the year that:

1) everyone is allowed to make mistakes, including the teacher,

2) all students are encouraged to take risks and try new things, and

3) no one is allowed to laugh at or humiliate another person.

Q "If you think you can do it, then try. If you try, that's the only way to succeed" *-Walt Disney*

1977

"And now for something completely different."

㉞ Maintain a Sense of Humor

Probably some of the best advice I ever received was
from my first master teacher, John McFall. John
taught 5th grade and his class loved him. He was
intelligent, very organized, and funny . . . a natural.
During the second week of my assignment as a
student teacher, John took me to lunch. During lunch
he shared several valuable teaching tips he'd learned
over the previous ten years, but one tip he shared

stuck with me forever, and that was this: **Never lose your sense of humor**. No matter how crazy things get in the classroom or how difficult a particular student or parent or principal can be at times, never get so lost that you lose your sense of humor. If you want to truly make a difference in your students' lives and continue to enjoy teaching everyday, you've got to be able to laugh at yourself and all the junk that's not important.

Laughter makes people feel better. Laughter helps reduce stress.

Did you laugh today?

Q "The most wasted of all days is one without laughter." -*e.e. cummings*

㉟ Morning Chuckle

A guy is sitting quietly reading his paper when his wife sneaks up behind him and whacks him on the head with a frying pan. "What was that for?" he says.

"That was for the piece of paper in your pants pocket with the name Mary Lou written on it," she shrieks.

"Wait, Hon, I can explain!" he pleads. "Two weeks ago when I went to the races, Mary Lou was the name of one of the horses I bet on." She looks satisfied, apologizes, and goes off to do work around the house.

Three days later he's again sitting in his chair reading when she nails him with an even bigger frying pan, knocking him out cold. When he comes to, he screams, "What the heck was that for?"

"Your horse phoned."

Funny story, huh . . . but, what's the point?

Let your students find the point.

- Be honest.

- Don't lie.

- What goes around, comes around.

- Don't take advantage of people, especially if you love them.

- Don't hurt people.

You're dealing with children. Be a healthy role model and take that responsibility seriously. Remember, they watch and they learn. Oh yeah, one more thing, don't forget to laugh.

(36) Takes Pictures of Your Students Working Together

Students love pictures of themselves and their friends together. They won't admit it, but they do. Get an inexpensive digital camera and start snapping. I took pictures while they were working in groups or on a project and then again when they did their group presentations for their final grade. I arranged them creatively on the back board and they were an instant hit. Once the word got out I suddenly had students from other classes stopping by after school to view the photos.

One year I left the photos up for Open House. Wow . . . you would have thought I just discovered the Fountain of Youth. Parents were thrilled and very insistent that I save the pictures for them. Naturally, all pictures were duplicated and sent home with each student. Every year from then on I made sure I designed a pictorial display for Open House, highlighting the students engaged in significant activities during that school year.

> **BONUS**
>
> Videotaping works great, also. Videotape various activities, edit the tape, and show it at Open House, <u>or</u> show it to your students at the end of the year as a surprise.

Smile . . . and say, "Cheese!"

*Don't forget to put yourself in the picture. There are lots of great student photographers that would love the experience.

NOTES

37 Be Prepared for Interruptions

You're in the middle of the best lecture you've ever given. The material is flowing, and your timing is perfect. If this keeps up you could be considered for teacher of the year. The place is rockin' with questions and the vice principal comes on the loud speaker declaring to God and country that the school is officially on rainy-day schedule. Suddenly this golden moment is lost and learning has been put on mute. You watch in disbelief as some other teacher receives the Oscar for BEST LESSON EVER.

Don't panic.

Unfortunately, interruptions like this one occur and cannot be avoided. You take a deep breath and venture on. It's been my experience that most students don't worry about interruptions as much as most teachers do. An exciting, well-planned lesson will prevail and the learning you have started will continue.

FLASH!
Have a Plan B – Be flexible

SUGGESTION:

If you experience many interruptions during one period or morning, then share this frustration with your mentor teacher. Chances are they are also not happy about the stop and start process, and will hopefully bring it to the attention of the administration.

Memorize
Your
School's
Emergency
Plan

Q "When you fall into the river, you're no longer a fisherman-you're a swimmer." *-Author Unknown*

"Don't forget to be 'fore' every student."

③⑧ Occasionally Do an Activity That's Just for Fun

I prided myself at being a master of time on task. My students were trained from Day 1 to check the agenda on the board each day as they entered the room, and then to get busy immediately. I knew the amount of material we had to cover that year, so every minute became very valuable.

But, if you're like me, every so often you need a break in the action. Even with the variety I provided within the lessons, my students needed a time out. I was never a huge proponent of unstructured free time, so I taught them Human Bingo and the Unmatch Game. They loved these games. But the best part was these games required only five to fifteen minutes to play. I'm a big fan of Simon Says, so occasionally I'd play a round to see if they could beat me. They never did.

Regardless of the activity, game or movie you choose as a well-earned break, the students will appreciate it, and look forward to it in the future.

Q "All work and no play makes Jack a dull boy."

- Proverb

(39) Human Bingo

Human Bingo is played exactly like regular Bingo except you use names instead of numbers. It's fun, it's exciting, and students genuinely cheer when they hear a classmate's name.

Here's how to play:

• Give each student a sheet of scratch paper
(*one side needs to be blank*)

• On the blank side have them design a bingo card that has three lines down and three lines across (*16 squares*).

	Bill		

Use a full 8 1/2 x 11 sheet

NOTE:
You can use two lines both directions for 9 squares or four lines both directions for 25 squares. I found 16 squares worked best for me because it fit my block of time.

The lines don't have to be perfectly straight.

- Have them <u>print</u> their first name in any square. If you have two or more students with the same first name, then have them print the first initial of their last names also.

- When you say, "Go!", the students get up and have 15 other students print their first names in one of the boxes.

NOTE:
Students cannot print other students' names in their boxes. They must have another student print his/her name in the box. If they break this rule, then they are disqualified from playing. It's about trust.

- When their card is complete, they are to return to their seat and wait for the beginning of the game.

- Once you have everyone seated with a completed card, you randomly call out your students' names. (*I use my roll book or my seating chart*).

- Students are not allowed to call out names they need to make bingo.

- If the student has the name that's been called out, then he/she puts a big X through that box.

- The first student to have all four boxes X'd either across, down, diagonally, or the four corners, then he/she screams out, "Bingo!"

(Note: You can only have one winner for each possibility. For example, once the first student wins 'across', then across is gone and no one else can get "Bingo" for across during that game. However, ties are ok. If two or more students scream, "Bingo!" on the same name, and they truly have Bingo, then they are all rewarded as winners.)

This is a wonderful game because students get to interact with one another. They also get an opportunity to get up and move around the classroom. Not only does every student get to participate, but every time a student's name is called, people cheer. This game requires a minimum of 15 minutes to complete. You can use it as an ice breaker, a reward, or if you have unforeseen schedule changes and one class ends up a little longer than normal.

NOTES

Time flies when you're having fun.

④⓪ Keep a Journal

I pride myself on having a pretty good memory. With all the variables involved in teaching multiple subjects and classes, I think it's definitely a requirement for effective teaching. However, I don't think any teacher has the capability to remember every incredible lesson, every incredible student, or for that fact, all the weird, awkward things that occur in any classroom during one complete school year.

So, keep a journal. It can be a notebook, a composition book, or just lined paper in a binder. It provides you with a place where you can record memorable events, activities that worked (or didn't work), and notes and thoughts you found important for that year.

It's not something you write in every day. It's something you write in when you want to . . . something to write in once a week. The number of times you write in your journal is up to you. The value of this exercise lies in the fact that you have a recorded history of that particular year from which you can reminisce, learn, change, and grow.

"It's my room and I'll cry if I want to."

It's been one of those days. The copy machine broke down this morning leaving you one important ditto short . . . the bulb in your overhead projector blew and there's no replacement . . . Bobby in 4th period is being overly needy today, and . . .

it's probably time for
REFLECTION

 Try this.

Keep a record of the day's events. At the end of the day or when you get home, sit down and reflect on the day. Jot down what worked, what didn't work, observations, questions, thoughts . . . like a journal. It doesn't need to be elaborate and it shouldn't be laborious. You'll be surprised at how much this simple task helps with planning for next year. Besides, you'll read this again in five years and be amazed at how much you've grown as a teacher.

Write
It
Down

(41) Most Improved

Most schools award a student or students for being most improved.

Most schools are configured into teams that award a student or students for being most improved.

Most teachers select a student or students and award them the honor of being most improved.

. . . but most teachers deserve this award – each and every year.

Each trimester after grades go home, each of our seven teams would host their own awards assembly. The categories were pretty consistent with other schools: principal's honor roll, honor roll, 4.0's, outstanding behavior, perfect attendance, etc. We also awarded students for being most improved. These were the students who had demonstrated amazing progress in either academics or behavior. This award not only supported the types of behavior we expected in class, but it also gave the other students the opportunity to choose that goal for themselves.

It dawned on me that the teachers who truly deserved an award for "most improved" each year are the same ones who were the real educational leaders. They have a strong classroom management program, a challenging academic program, a love for their students, a sense of humor, and a desire to be the best.

They're flexible, knowledgeable, and students love being in their classrooms.

Good teachers are always growing and learning like their students, consistently striving for the best learning environment they can design. There's no doubt in my mind that they all deserve the highest honor for being "Most Improved."

Because of this belief, I created, "Mr. B's Most Improved Teacher of the Week." At the time we had staff meetings every Tuesday, and most of the time they were not that exciting. So in order to provide a positive lift to this activity, I awarded one teacher each week with this award. It was hugely popular with both the staff and the administration. The following year, as part of each weekly staff meeting, the principal singled out specific staff members and applauded them for a contribution they had made that week.

㊷ Final Thoughts

1. Reward good behavior.

2. Reward good work habits.

3. Reward yourself.

4. Don't hold grudges.

5. Never forget they're children.

6. Have fun every day.

7. Laugh every day.

8. Believe in yourself.

9. Challenge yourself.

10. Did I answer all your questions?

   If I didn't, and I mean this sincerely,
   go to my website and ask me the question.
   www.billbaileyproductions.com
   Or, for that matter, ask me any question you
   have concerning teaching, and I'll attempt to
   provide an answer. Remember, you're here
   today, planning for tomorrow, so a child's
   future will be rewarding and successful.

 "Happiness is a journey, not a destination. Work like you don't need money, love like you have never been hurt, and dance like no one is watching.." *-Author Unknown*

NOTES

NOTES

NOTES